## BIRD VIEWING AREAS

1. Sungei Buloh Bird Sanctuary
2. Cameron Highlands & Fraser's Hill
3. Taman Negara National Park
4. Mount Kinabalu National Park
5. Niah National Park
6. Bali Balat National Park
7. Mount Polis
8. St. Paul's Subterranean River National Park
9. Khao Yai National Park
10. Kaeng Krachan National Park
11. Na Hin Forest
12. Luang Prabang
13. Sierra Madre
14. Mount Kitanglad Range Natural Park
15. Tam Dao National Park
16. Cát Tiên National Park
17. Southern Mekong River
18. Chu Yang Sin National Park
19. Inle Wetland Wildlife Sanctuary
20. Bukit Barisan Selatan National Park
21. Peradayan Forest Reserve
22. Kerinci-Seblat National Park
23. Sabangau National Park
24. Lore Lindu National Park

Text and illustrations © 2015, 2017 by Waterford Press Inc. All rights reserved. Cover images © Shutterstock.

Waterford Press produces reference guides that introduce novices to nature, science, travel and languages. Publisher information is featured on the website: www.waterfordpress.com

To order, call 800-434-2555. For permissions, or to share comments, e-mail editor@waterfordpress.com. For information on custom-published products, call 800-434-2555 or e-mail info@waterfordpress.com.   610326

ISBN 978-1-58355-961-1   $7.95 U.S.

# SOUTHEAST ASIA BIRDS

## A Folding Pocket Guide to Familiar Species

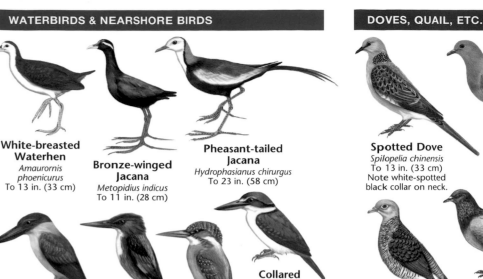

Scan for more info

Made in the USA

SOUTHEAST ASIA BIRDS – A Folding Pocket Guide to Familiar Species   Kavanagh/Leung

---

## WATERBIRDS & NEARSHORE BIRDS

**Little Grebe**
*Tachybaptus ruficollis*
To 12 in. (30 cm)
Also called red-throated little grebe.

**Common Pintail**
*Anas acuta*  To 30 in. (75 cm)

**Common Teal**
*Anas crecca*  To 16 in. (40 cm)

**Lesser Whistling-Duck**
*Dendrocygna javanica*
To 16 in. (40 cm)

**Spot-billed Duck**
*Anas poecilorhyncha*
To 2 ft. (60 cm)

**Garganey**
*Anas querquedula*
To 15 in. (38 cm)
Note white eyebrow.

**Great Egret**
*Ardea alba*
To 38 in. (95 cm)
Note yellow bill and black feet.

**Grey Heron**
*Ardea cinerea*
To 38 in. (95 cm)

**Black-crowned Night-Heron**
*Nycticorax nycticorax*
To 28 in. (70 cm)

**Little Egret**
*Egretta garzetta*
To 26 in. (65 cm)
Note black bill and yellow feet.

**Little Heron**
*Butorides striatus*
To 14 in. (35 cm)
Note black cap.

**Chinese Pond Heron**
*Ardeola bacchus*
To 18 in. (45 cm)

**Asian Openbill**
*Anastomus oscitans*
To 32 in. (80 cm)
Bill does not close tightly.

**Cattle Egret**
*Bubulcus ibis*
To 20 in. (50 cm)

---

## WATERBIRDS & NEARSHORE BIRDS

**Sarus Crane**
*Grus antigone*
To 6 ft. (1.8 m)
The world's tallest flying bird is a rare resident in Cambodia and Vietnam.

**Black-headed Ibis**
*Threskiornis melanocephala*
To 32 in. (80 cm)

**Painted Stork**
*Mycteria leucocephala*
To 40 in. (1 m)

**Black-winged Stilt**
*Himantopus himantopus*
To 15 in. (38 cm)

**Redshank**
*Tringa totanus*
To 12 in. (30 cm)
Note red legs.

**Common Snipe**
*Gallinago gallinago*
To 12 in. (30 cm)

**Lesser Sand Plover**
*Charadrius mongolus*
To 8 in. (20 cm)

**Little Ringed Plover**
*Charadrius dubius*
To 6 in. (15 cm)

**Red-necked Stint**
*Calidris ruficollis*
To 6 in. (15 cm)

**Common Sandpiper**
*Tringa hypoleucos*
To 8 in. (20 cm)
Plumage is rich brown above and white below.

**Red-wattled Lapwing**
*Vanellus indicus*
To 14 in. (35 cm)

**Pacific Golden Plover**
*Pluvialis fulva*
To 11 in. (28 cm)

**Whimbrel**
*Numenius phaeopus*
To 20 in. (50 cm)
Note striped crown.

**Sanderling**
*Calidris alba*
To 8 in. (20 cm)
Runs in and out with waves along shorelines.

Non-breeding plumage

---

## WATERBIRDS & NEARSHORE BIRDS

**White-breasted Waterhen**
*Amaurornis phoenicurus*
To 13 in. (33 cm)

**Bronze-winged Jacana**
*Metopidius indicus*
To 11 in. (28 cm)

**Pheasant-tailed Jacana**
*Hydrophasianus chirurgus*
To 23 in. (58 cm)

**Stork-billed Kingfisher**
*Pelargopsis capensis*
To 19 in. (38 cm)
Note large size.

**White-throated Kingfisher**
*Halcyon smyrnensis*
To 9 in. (23 cm)

**Common Kingfisher**
*Alcedo atthis*
To 7 in. (18 cm)

**Collared Kingfisher**
*Halcyon chloris*
To 10 in. (25 cm)

**Pied Kingfisher**
*Ceryle rudis*
To 10 in. (25 cm)

**Great Frigatebird**
*Fregata minor*
To 40 in. (1 m)
Note red throat, long wingspan and forked tail. Females have a white throat.

**Common Gallinule**
*Gallinula chloropus*
To 14 in. (35 cm)

**Common Coot**
*Fulica atra*
To 16 in. (40 cm)

**Little Cormorant**
*Microcarbo niger*
To 20 in. (50 cm)

**Purple Swamphen**
*Porphyrio porphyrio*
To 18 in. (45 cm)

**Whiskered Tern**
*Chlidonias hybrida*
To 11 in. (28 cm)

**Brown-headed Gull**
*Larus brunnicephalus*
To 18 in. (45 cm)

---

## DOVES, QUAIL, ETC.

**Spotted Dove**
*Spilopelia chinensis*
To 13 in. (33 cm)
Note white-spotted black collar on neck.

**Pink-necked Green Pigeon**
*Treron vernans*
To 10 in. (25 cm)

**Green Imperial Pigeon**
*Ducula aenea*
To 19 in. (48 cm)

**Zebra Dove**
*Geopelia striata*
To 8 in. (20 cm)
Note small size and barred flanks.

**Rock Pigeon**
*Columba livia*
To 13 in. (33 cm)

**Mountain Imperial Pigeon**
*Ducula badia*
To 18 in. (45 cm)
Wings and back are brownish.

**Emerald Dove**
*Chalcophaps indica*
To 10 in. (25 cm)

**Oriental Turtle-Dove**
*Streptopelia orientalis*
To 13 in. (33 cm)
Note neck stripes.

**Red Turtle-Dove**
*Streptopelia tranquebarica*
To 9 in. (23 cm)

**Great Argus**
*Argusianus argus*
To 4 ft. (1.2 m)

**Red Junglefowl**
*Gallus gallus*
To 30 in. (75 cm)

**Crested Wood-Partridge**
*Rollulus roulroul*
To 10 in. (25 cm)

**Blue-breasted Quail**
*Coturnix chinensis*
To 6 in. (15 cm)

**Barred Buttonquail**
*Turnix suscitator*
To 7 in. (18 cm)

## BIRDS OF PREY

**Black Kite**
*Milvus migrans*
To 22 in. (55 cm)

**Common Buzzard**
*Buteo buteo*
To 22 in. (55 cm)
Plumage may be
dark or light brown.

**Osprey**
*Pandion haliaetus*
To 2 ft. (60 cm)
Fish-eating raptor.

**Brahminy Kite**
*Haliastur indus*
To 19 in. (48 cm)

**Crested Serpent Eagle**
*Spilornis cheela*
To 30 in. (75 cm)
Note black head crest.

**White-bellied Sea Eagle**
*Haliaeetus leucogaster*
To 34 in. (85 cm)
Resident in
coastal areas.

**Crested Honey Buzzard**
*Pernis ptilorhynchus*
To 26 in. (65 cm)
Note small head and
short crest.

**Black-shouldered Kite**
*Elanus caeruleus*
To 14 in. (35 cm)
Note all-white tail.

**Crested Goshawk**
*Accipiter trivirgatus*
To 18 in. (45 cm)

**Shikra**
*Accipiter badius*
To 12 in. (30 cm)

**Brown Hawk Owl**
*Ninox scutulata*
To 12 in. (30 cm)

**Eurasian Kestrel**
*Falco tinnunculus*
To 12 in. (30 cm)

**Barn Owl**
*Tyto alba*
To 20 in. (50 cm)
Note heart-
shaped face.

**Collared Scops-Owl**
*Otus lempiji*
To 9 in. (23 cm)

## BEE-EATERS, TROGONS, ETC.

**Blue-throated Bee-eater**
*Merops viridis*
To 11 in. (28 cm)

**Chestnut-headed Bee-eater**
*Merops leschenaulti*
To 8 in. (20 cm)

**Blue-tailed Bee-eater**
*Merops philippinus*
To 12 in. (30 cm)

**Green Bee-eater**
*Merops orientalis*
To 7 in. (18 cm)

**Whiskered Treeswift**
*Hemiprocne comata*
To 6 in. (15 cm)

**Red-headed Trogon**
*Harpactes erythrocephalus*
To 13 in. (33 cm)

**Scarlet-rumped Trogon**
*Harpactes duvaucelii*
To 10 in. (25 cm)

**Indian Roller**
*Coracias benghalensis*
To 11 in. (28 cm)

**Crested Hoopoe**
*Upupa epops*
To 12 in. (30 cm)
Head crest is erect when
alarmed. Call is a soft
repeated – *hoop-hoop*.

**Vernal Hanging Parrot**
*Loriculus vernalis*
To 5 in. (13 cm)

**House Swift**
*Apus affinis*
To 5 in.
(13 cm)

**Coppersmith Barbet**
*Megalaima haemacephala*
To 7 in. (18 cm)
Repetitive call – *tuk-tuk-tuk* –
has been likened to a
hammer striking metal.

**Green-billed Malkoha**
*Phaenicophaeus tristis*
To 22 in. (55 cm)

**Large-tailed Nightjar**
*Caprimulgus macrurus*
To 12 in. (30 cm)

**Green-eared Barbet**
*Megalaima faiostricta*
To 10 in. (25 cm)
Note green ear coverts.

## HORNBILLS, WOODPECKERS, ETC.

**Great Hornbill**
*Buceros bicornis*
To 42 in. (1.1 m)

**Oriental Pied Hornbill**
*Anthracoceros albirostris*
To 28 in. (70 cm)

**Wreathed Hornbill**
*Rhyticeros undulatus*
To 40 in. (1 m)

**Rufous Woodpecker**
*Celeus brachyurus*
To 10 in. (25 cm)

**Rhinoceros hornbill**
*Buceros rhinoceros*
To 4 ft. (1.2 m)

**Greater Goldenback**
*Chrysocolaptes guttacristatus*
To 13 in. (33 cm)

**Common Goldenback**
*Dinopium javanense*
To 12 in. (30 cm)

**Asian Koel**
*Eudynamys scolopaceus*
To 18 in. (45 cm)
Note red eyes.

**Indian Cuckoo**
*Cuculus micropterus*
To 13 in. (33 cm)

**Greater Coucal**
*Centropus sinensis*
To 19 in. (48 cm)
The similar lesser coucal
(*C. bengalensis*) is smaller.

**Dollarbird**
*Eurystomus orientalis*
To 12 in. (30 cm)
Named for the light,
coin-shaped patches
near its wingtips.

**Drongo Cuckoo**
*Surniculus lugubris*
To 10 in. (25 cm)

### PERCHING BIRDS

**Black-and-Red Broadbill**
*Cymbirhynchus macrorhynchos*
To 10 in. (25 cm)

**Silver-breasted Broadbill**
*Serilophus lunatus*
To 6 in. (15 cm)

**Black-and-Yellow Broadbill**
*Eurylaimus ochromalus*
To 6 in. (15 cm)

## PERCHING BIRDS

**Grey Wagtail**
*Motacilla cinerea*
To 8 in. (20 cm)
Note black throat
and long tail.

**Long-tailed Shrike**
*Lanius schach*
To 10 in. (25 cm)

**Brown Shrike**
*Lanius cristatus*
To 8 in. (20 cm)

**Hooded Pitta**
*Pitta steerii*
To 7 in. (18 cm)

**Great Tit**
*Parus major*
To 6 in. (15 cm)
Note black stripe
down center
of breast.

**Scarlet Minivet**
*Pericrocotus flammeus*
To 8 in. (20 cm)

**Blue-winged Pitta**
*Pitta moluccensis*
To 8 in. (20 cm)

**Pacific Swallow**
*Hirundo tahitica*
To 5 in. (13 cm)

**Red-rumped Swallow**
*Hirundo daurica*
To 7 in. (18 cm)

**Black-naped Monarch**
*Hypothymis azurea*
To 6 in. (15 cm)

**Black-naped Oriole**
*Oriolus chinensis*
To 11 in. (28 cm)

**Common Tailorbird**
*Orthotomus sutorius*
To 5.5 in. (14 cm)
Familiar backyard
species.

**Blue Rock Thrush**
*Monticola solitarius*
To 9 in. (23 cm)

**Asian Fairy Bluebird**
*Irena puella*
To 10 in. (25 cm)

**Black-hooded Oriole**
*Oriolus xanthornus*
To 10 in. (25 cm)

## PERCHING BIRDS

**Common Myna**
*Acridotheres tristis*
To 9 in. (23 cm)

**Common Hill Myna**
*Gracula religiosa*
To 12 in. (30 cm)

**Javan Myna**
*Acridotheres javanicus*
To 10 in. (25 cm)

**Yellow-vented Bulbul**
*Pycnonotus goiavier*
To 8 in. (20 cm)

**Red-whiskered Bulbul**
*Pycnonotus jocosus*
To 7 in. (18 cm)

**White-throated Fantail**
*Rhipidura albicollis*
To 8 in. (20 cm)
Active and restless,
it fans its tail when
perching.

**House Crow**
*Corvus splendens*
To 16 in. (40 cm)

**Oriental White-eye**
*Zosterops palpebrosus*
To 4 in. (10 cm)

**Oriental Magpie-Robin**
*Copsychus saularis*
To 7.5 in. (19 cm)

**Common Iora**
*Aegithina tiphia*
To 6 in. (15 cm)

**Little Spiderhunter**
*Arachnothera longirostra*
To 6 in. (15 cm)

**Eurasian Tree Sparrow**
*Passer montanus*
To 6 in. (15 cm)

**Crested Jay**
*Platylophus galericulatus*
To 13 in. (33 cm)

**Red Avadavat**
*Amandava amandava*
To 4 in. (10 cm)

**Scarlet-backed Flowerpecker**
*Dicaeum cruentatum*
To 4 in. (10 cm)

**Asian Pied Starling**
*Sturnus contra*
To 9 in. (23 cm)

## PERCHING BIRDS

**Asian Paradise Flycatcher**
*Terpsiphone paradisi*
To 30 in. (75 cm)
Plumage of male varies
from white to rufous.
Female is rufous.

**Scaly-breasted Munia**
*Lonchura punctulata*
To 4 in. (10 cm)

**White-rumped Munia**
*Lonchura striata*
To 4 in. (10 cm)

**Asian Glossy Starling**
*Aplonis panayensis*
To 8 in. (20 cm)

**Streaked Weaver**
*Ploceus manyar*
To 5 in. (13 cm)

**Olive-backed Sunbird**
*Nectarinia jugularis*
To 4 in. (10 cm)

**Chestnut Munia**
*Lonchura malacca*
To 4 in. (10 cm)

**Brown-throated Sunbird**
*Anthreptes malacensis*
To 6 in. (15 cm)

**Purple Sunbird**
*Nectarinia asiatica*
To 4 in. (10 cm)

**Crimson Sunbird**
*Aethopyga siparaja*
To 4 in. (10 cm)

**Asian Golden Weaver**
*Ploceus hypoxanthus*
To 6 in. (15 cm)

**Black Drongo**
*Dicrurus macrocercus*
To 11 in. (28 cm)
Note white spot
near beak.

**Greater Racket-tailed Drongo**
*Dicrurus paradiseus*
To 26 in. (65 cm)
Tail 'rackets' can
equal the body
length.